CHILDREN'S AUTHORS

SUZANNE COLLINS

Jill C. Wheeler

ABDO Publishing Company

visit us at
www.abdopublishing.com

Printed in the United States of America, North Mankato, Minnesota.
102012
012013

 PRINTED ON RECYCLED PAPER

Cover Photo: AP Images
Interior Photos: AP Images pp. 5, 7, 9, 11, 17, 21; Corbis p. 20
    Jacket illustration copyright © 2003 by Daniel Craig from GREGOR THE OVERLANDER
    by Suzanne Collins. Scholastic Inc./Scholastic Press. Used by Permission. p. 13
    Jacket illustration copyright © 2008 by Tim O'Brien from THE HUNGER GAMES
    by Suzanne Collins. Scholastic Inc./Scholastic Press. Used by Permission. p. 15
    Jacket illustration copyright © 2009 by Tim O'Brien from CATCHING FIRE
    by Suzanne Collins. Scholastic Inc./Scholastic Press. Used by permission. p. 16
    Jacket illustration copyright © 2010 by Tim O'Brien from MOCKINGJAY
    by Suzanne Collins. Scholastic Inc./Scholastic Press. Used by Permission. p. 19

Series Coordinator: Megan M. Gunderson / Editors: Tamara L. Britton, Stephanie Hedlund
Art Direction: Neil Klinepier

Cataloging-in-Publication Data

Wheeler, Jill C., 1964-
 Suzanne Collins / Jill C. Wheeler.
  p. cm. -- (Children's authors)
Includes bibliographical references and index.
ISBN 978-1-61783-574-2
1. Collins, Suzanne, 1962- --Juvenile literature. 2.Authors, American--21st century--Biography--Juvenile literature. 3. Women authors, American--21st century--Biography--Juvenile literature. 4. Children's stories--Authorship--Juvenile literature. I. Title.
813/.6--dc23
[B]
               2012946381

CONTENTS

Hungry for More

Like many authors, Suzanne Collins writes about topics that interest her. Unlike many young adult authors, she writes about violence and war.

Collins is the best-selling author of the Hunger Games **trilogy**. These **dystopian** books are set in a futuristic society. Every year, that society forces 24 young people to fight to the death. They do so in an event called the Hunger Games.

In all, the trilogy has sold more than 50 million copies. The titles were on the *New York Times* best-seller list for more than three years. And, Collins became the best-selling author of all time for Amazon.com's Kindle titles.

The Hunger Games series has encouraged many readers to pick up a book. It has drawn in both male and female readers of all ages. And, it has started a lively discussion about reality television and violence.

Collins had a successful career as a television writer before she turned to novels. She was 41 years old when her first novel was published. Ever since, readers have fallen in love with her characters and been hooked by her plots.

Collins's stories are described as adventure, science fiction, and fantasy. But, she considers them war stories above all.

MILITARY KID

Suzanne Collins was born in August of 1962 in New Jersey. She was the youngest of four children born to Michael and Jane Collins. Suzanne had two older sisters and an older brother.

Suzanne's father was an officer in the U.S. Air Force. So, her family moved often while she was growing up. Suzanne's father also taught military history at the U.S. Military Academy at West Point, New York. Some of Suzanne's earliest memories include watching soldiers performing drills at this school.

Suzanne's father shared his military interests with his family. When touring battlefields, they didn't just talk about the battle. They discussed what led up to it and what happened as a result.

The Collins family moved to Indiana in 1968. That same year, Suzanne's father left to serve in the **Vietnam War**. Suzanne spent many days wondering where her father was and when he was coming home.

At age 11, Suzanne enjoyed solitary activities such as reading. She also enjoyed gymnastics and playing in the woods with her friends.

The Collins family saw news coverage of the war on television. It was frightening, but they talked openly about what they saw. Suzanne grew up understanding that war was just one more part of life. Many years later, this influenced her writing.

A Love of Literature

Suzanne's father eventually returned from Vietnam. Five years later, the family moved to Brussels, Belgium. There, Suzanne attended fifth and sixth grade. She vividly remembers her English teacher, Miss Vance.

Miss Vance would read Edgar Allan Poe stories to interested students. Suzanne loved to hear "The Tell-Tale Heart" or "The Masque of the Red Death." Some might think those stories are not appropriate for young listeners. Yet Suzanne appreciated them.

Suzanne loved literature. Some of her favorite stories were from Greek mythology. One was the story of **Theseus and the Minotaur**. Suzanne was fascinated by the ancient story of the **gladiator** Spartacus, too. Suzanne also discovered she loved acting. Beginning around age 12, she performed in many plays.

By the time Suzanne entered high school, her family had moved to another new city. She attended the Alabama

School of Fine Arts in Birmingham. There, she studied theater arts. And, she continued to explore literature.

Suzanne's favorite books addressed social issues. One of these was *1984* by George Orwell. Others included Leo Tolstoy's *Anna Karenina* and William Golding's *Lord of the Flies*.

Growing up, Suzanne also enjoyed reading A Wrinkle in Time *by Madeleine L'Engle and* The Phantom Tollbooth *by Norton Juster.*

TV WRITER

Suzanne graduated from high school in 1980. She continued her education at Indiana University in Bloomington. While there, she met an acting student named Cap Pryor. The two fell in love and eventually married.

While in college, Suzanne studied theater and telecommunications. She decided she was more interested in writing **scripts** than in acting them out. The decision led her to write her first one-act play.

Suzanne graduated from college in 1985. Two years later, she moved to New York City. There, she earned a master of fine arts degree in dramatic writing from New York University.

After earning her master's degree, Suzanne began a successful career writing for children's television. She worked on the Nickelodeon programs *Clarissa Explains It All*, *Wow! Wow! Wubbzy!*, and *The Mystery Files of Shelby Woo*. She

Suzanne and her husband have two children. Their son is named Charlie, and their daughter is named Isabel.

also worked her way up to be head writer for the public television series *Clifford's Puppy Days*.

Suzanne also wrote for an animated show called *Generation O!* It aired in 2000. During this time, Suzanne met children's book author James Proimos. He encouraged her to try writing fiction. After much thought, she decided to do just that. She began writing what would be her first published novel.

Rats, Bats, and Cockroaches

Collins had a big year in 2003. She and her family left New York City to live in Connecticut. And, her first book was published!

Gregor the Overlander is about an 11-year-old boy living in New York City. One day, he discovers a secret human society hidden beneath the city. The secret society features everything from talking cockroaches to a giant evil rat leader.

To write the book, Collins dived into research. She read all about rats, bats, spiders, and cockroaches. She also had to learn how to write descriptions. In her television job, she wrote **dialogue** and action descriptions. Writing a novel is quite different. For example, writing the description of the underground city of Regalia took a long time!

While writing *Gregor*, Collins sometimes called her father for help. She asked him which military **strategies** would make sense. Sadly, Michael Collins died before his daughter's first book was published.

Gregor the Overlander became the first of five books in the Underland Chronicles series. The series featured themes not typically found in children's books. These included death, loss, violence, and war. However, the series was well received.

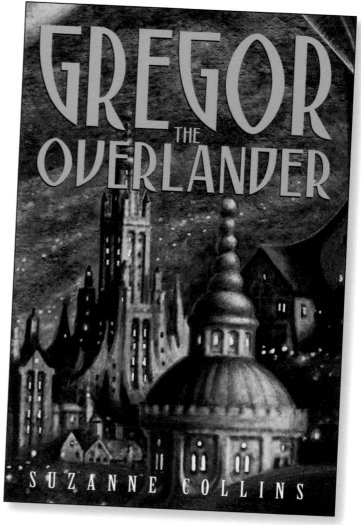

Gregor was inspired by the story of Alice in Wonderland. Yet unlike Alice, Gregor lives in the city. Collins felt modern readers would be more familiar with that setting than the countryside.

WAR FOR KIDS

The inspiration for Collins's next series came suddenly. One night while watching television, she came across a reality program. It featured young people competing against each other for money. As Collins sleepily flipped channels, she saw young soldiers fighting in the war in Iraq. The images blurred together, and *The Hunger Games* was born.

This new fantasy series takes place in a future world called Panem. Each year, Panem's cruel adult leaders force young contestants to fight to the death.

Like today's reality program viewers, the people of Panem follow the games on television. Much like the story of **Theseus and the Minotaur**, the children in *The Hunger Games* are sacrificed for their homelands. And like Spartacus, heroine Katniss Everdeen changes from a would-be victim into a rebel leader.

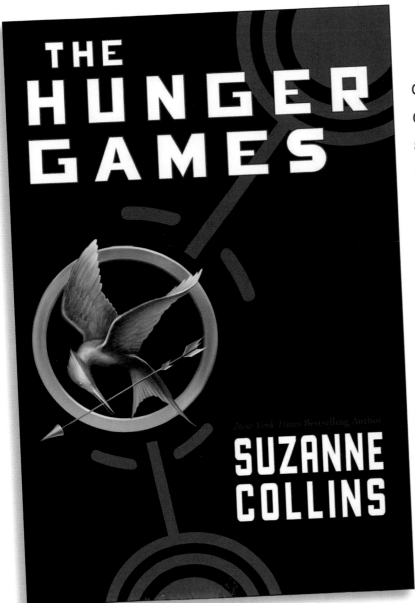

Collins continued writing children's television **scripts** even as she brought the terrifying story of Panem to life. It was often a relief to work on a light-hearted script such as *Wubbzy*. At least that way, she knew all the characters would still be alive at the end of the show. That was not the case for *The Hunger Games*!

Katniss's story is similar to that of Spartacus. She is a slave, a gladiator, a rebel, and the face of a war.

A Phenomenon

Scholastic published *The Hunger Games* in 2008. Collins followed the book with the **sequel** *Catching Fire* in 2009. She concluded the **dystopian trilogy** in 2010's *Mockingjay*. *Mockingjay* sold some 450,000 printed and electronic copies in just its first week of publication. The series was so popular that Collins was named one of *TIME* magazine's 100 most influential people in 2010. The first book was made into a movie, which

The Second Book of THE HUNGER GAMES

CATCHING FIRE

New York Times Bestselling Author
SUZANNE COLLINS

Catching Fire will also be a movie. Mockingjay will be split into two films.

16

Jennifer Lawrence stars in **The Hunger Games** *as Katniss Everdeen.*

was released in March 2012. Collins participated in casting her vivid characters. She also helped writer and director Gary Ross with the **script**. When the movie premiered, it was wildly successful. It earned $152.2 million on its opening weekend!

On the Defense

Collins has been criticized for writing young adult books with such violent content. But she defends her work. Collins says it is important that young people talk about and understand difficult subjects such as violence and war.

Collins also points out that her stories are not new. Ancient **gladiators** lived a real-life version of the Hunger Games. They lived under the control of a ruthless government. They were forced to fight to the death. And perhaps most strikingly, their battles were entertainment for an audience.

Collins also believes it is important to help young people become more critical of the media. She believes young children cannot tell the difference between what is real and what is not real. Yet kids have to be able to tell the difference between a news report and a fake television show.

Collins also is careful to help her readers work up to particularly dramatic scenes. Both Gregor and Katniss face increasingly tough challenges as their stories progress. Readers are asked to grow with the characters as the story moves along.

The Final Book of THE HUNGER GAMES

MOCKINGJAY

New York Times Bestselling Author

SUZANNE COLLINS

Collins wrote the Gregor books for readers ages 9 to 12. The Hunger Games trilogy is aimed at readers 12 and up.

WHAT'S NEXT

Today, Collins lives in Sandy Hook, Connecticut. She shares her home with her family and two adopted stray cats. There, Collins may write three to five hours a day. She admits she likes working in her pajamas!

Collins keeps a low profile and grants few interviews. She prefers to work on her writing. In fact, she is already busy researching another young adult series.

In addition, Collins is exploring a children's book based on her father's military service. She hopes this book will be a memorial to her family.

Collins's home in Sandy Hook is about two hours north of New York City.

She also hopes it can help other kids whose parents have been sent to war in faraway places.

Collins's family and teachers always encouraged her interest in the arts. They never told her she could not make a living as a professional writer. Millions of fans have made that dream into a reality. Whatever she writes next, it is likely to keep fans talking and thinking!

Collins enjoyed writing as part of a group when she worked on television. But today, she also enjoys that she writes her books alone.

GLOSSARY

dialogue - a written conversation between two or more characters.

dystopian (dihs-TOH-pee-uhn) - relating to an imaginary place where people often fear for their lives.

gladiator - a person who fought to the death for public entertainment in ancient Rome.

script - the written words and directions used to put on a play, movie, or television show.

sequel - a book, movie, or other work that continues the story begun in a preceding one.

strategy - the planning of military operations.

Theseus and the Minotaur - characters in an ancient Greek myth. In the story, the people of Athens are forced by their enemies to send seven boys and seven girls into a maze. The maze is inhabited by a half-human, half-bull monster known as the Minotaur. Theseus defeats him.

trilogy - a series of three novels, movies, or other works that are closely related and involve the same characters or themes.

Vietnam War - from 1957 to 1975. A long, failed attempt by the United States to stop North Vietnam from taking over South Vietnam.

WEB SITES

To learn more about Suzanne Collins, visit ABDO Publishing Company online. Web sites about Suzanne Collins are featured on our Book Links page. These links are routinely monitored and updated to provide the most current information available.
www.abdopublishing.com

INDEX